EMMANUEL JOSEPH

Wired Destinies: The Personal Journeys
Behind Global Startups

Copyright © 2025 by Emmanuel Joseph

All rights reserved. No part of this publication may be reproduced, stored or transmitted in any form or by any means, electronic, mechanical, photocopying, recording, scanning, or otherwise without written permission from the publisher. It is illegal to copy this book, post it to a website, or distribute it by any other means without permission.

First edition

This book was professionally typeset on Reedsy.
Find out more at reedsy.com

Contents

1. Chapter 1: The Spark — 1
2. Chapter 2: Taking the Leap — 3
3. Chapter 3: Building the Foundation — 5
4. Chapter 4: Facing Adversity — 7
5. Chapter 5: The Growth Phase — 9
6. Chapter 6: Innovation and Adaptation — 11
7. Chapter 7: Building a Culture — 13
8. Chapter 8: The Role of Mentorship — 15
9. Chapter 9: Making a Social Impact — 17
10. Chapter 10: Navigating the Global Stage — 19
11. Chapter 11: The Exit Strategy — 21
12. Chapter 12: Reflections and Legacy — 23

1

Chapter 1: The Spark

In the vast realm of entrepreneurship, every groundbreaking startup begins with a single spark of inspiration. These sparks often stem from personal experiences, observations, or a deep-seated desire to solve a specific problem. For instance, Sarah, a young tech enthusiast, was frustrated with the inefficiency of public transportation in her city. This frustration led her to develop an app that optimized bus routes in real-time, eventually revolutionizing urban commuting. Similarly, Raj, inspired by his grandmother's struggle with traditional banking, founded a fintech startup that simplified financial transactions for the elderly. These stories underscore the idea that personal challenges often ignite the flames of innovation, pushing individuals to create solutions that have a global impact.

The journey from inspiration to execution is often fraught with uncertainty. Many entrepreneurs find themselves at a crossroads, contemplating whether to pursue their ideas full-time or maintain their current career paths. Jane, a corporate lawyer, faced this dilemma when she conceptualized an online platform for legal advice. Despite the security of her job, she decided to take the leap, driven by her passion to democratize access to legal services. Her story is a testament to the courage and determination required to transform a vision into reality.

Once the decision is made, the next step involves laying the groundwork for the startup. This phase is characterized by intense brainstorming, planning, and the creation of a minimal viable product (MVP). For Miguel, a graphic designer, the initial phase of his startup involved countless hours of sketching and prototyping a new design tool. He also assembled a small team of like-minded individuals who shared his vision. These foundational steps are crucial in shaping the future trajectory of the startup.

Challenges are an inevitable part of the startup journey. Entrepreneurs often encounter obstacles ranging from financial constraints to market competition. Emma, the founder of a health tech startup, faced significant hurdles when her initial product failed to gain traction. However, her resilience and willingness to pivot led to the development of a new product that addressed a critical gap in the market. Her story highlights the importance of perseverance and adaptability in overcoming adversity.

As startups gain initial traction, the focus shifts to scaling and growth. This phase involves strategic planning, securing funding, and expanding the team. For Alex, the founder of an e-commerce platform, the growth phase was marked by a successful series A funding round and the establishment of partnerships with major retailers. This period of expansion is a critical juncture where startups transition from small operations to larger enterprises, requiring meticulous execution and a clear vision.

In the fast-paced world of technology, continuous innovation and adaptation are essential for survival. Startups must remain agile, constantly iterating on their products and services to stay relevant. Nina, the founder of a social media platform, emphasizes the importance of listening to user feedback and staying ahead of industry trends. Her ability to adapt and innovate has kept her platform competitive in a rapidly evolving market. These stories of innovation underscore the dynamic nature of the startup landscape and the need for a forward-thinking approach.

2

Chapter 2: Taking the Leap

Taking the leap from ideation to implementation is often the most daunting step for aspiring entrepreneurs. This decision entails leaving behind the safety and security of conventional employment and diving into the uncertainties of startup life. For many, this transition is driven by a compelling desire to bring their vision to life. Take, for instance, David, a successful software engineer who left his lucrative job to develop an innovative educational platform. His unwavering belief in the power of technology to transform learning environments fueled his decision to take the plunge.

The initial phase of a startup journey is marked by both excitement and trepidation. Founders often face a myriad of challenges as they navigate uncharted waters. Jessica, who founded a sustainable fashion brand, recalls the sleepless nights spent planning her venture's launch. She grappled with fears of failure and the immense pressure to succeed. Yet, her passion for sustainable fashion and the support of her close-knit team kept her motivated. Her story illustrates the resilience and determination required to overcome the initial hurdles of entrepreneurship.

Financial constraints are a common challenge for many startups. Bootstrapping, seeking angel investors, or applying for grants are some of the ways entrepreneurs secure the necessary funding. Mark, the founder of a health-tech startup, initially funded his venture using his personal savings.

He later secured investment from a group of angel investors who believed in his vision. Mark's journey highlights the importance of resourcefulness and the ability to attract investors who share a common goal.

Another critical aspect of taking the leap is building a strong and capable team. Entrepreneurs must surround themselves with individuals who bring diverse skills and perspectives. Lisa, who co-founded a tech startup, emphasizes the value of collaboration and trust within her team. She carefully selected team members who were not only skilled but also shared her passion and vision. The synergy within her team was instrumental in overcoming challenges and driving the startup's success.

Taking the leap also involves a significant amount of risk. Entrepreneurs must be willing to embrace uncertainty and make decisions with limited information. Tom, the founder of a renewable energy startup, faced numerous setbacks and uncertainties in the early stages of his venture. However, his willingness to take calculated risks and learn from failures enabled him to navigate the complexities of the energy sector. His story underscores the importance of risk-taking and adaptability in the entrepreneurial journey.

The decision to take the leap is often accompanied by a deep sense of purpose. Entrepreneurs are driven by a desire to make a meaningful impact and bring positive change to society. Rachel, who founded a social enterprise, was motivated by her passion for addressing food insecurity in underserved communities. Her dedication to her mission inspired her to overcome obstacles and create a sustainable business model that provided nutritious meals to those in need. Rachel's journey highlights the profound sense of purpose that fuels entrepreneurs and drives them to persevere in the face of adversity.

3

Chapter 3: Building the Foundation

The initial stage of building a startup is akin to constructing the foundation of a skyscraper. Every element must be meticulously planned and executed to ensure stability and growth. For many entrepreneurs, this phase involves transforming an abstract idea into a tangible product or service. Emily, for example, began her journey by creating a basic prototype of her eco-friendly packaging solution. Her relentless focus on detail and quality laid the groundwork for what would later become a successful enterprise.

Assembling a strong team is paramount during the foundation phase. Entrepreneurs must seek out individuals who not only possess the necessary skills but also share their vision and values. When Leo started his tech startup, he carefully selected team members who were passionate about innovation and technology. This alignment in values and goals fostered a cohesive and motivated team, crucial for overcoming the inevitable challenges that lay ahead.

The development of a minimal viable product (MVP) is a critical step in the foundation phase. The MVP serves as a proof of concept, allowing entrepreneurs to test their ideas in the market with minimal resources. Julia, who founded a digital health platform, focused on creating an MVP that addressed the core needs of her target audience. By gathering feedback and iterating on her product, she was able to refine her offering and build a solid foundation for future growth.

Securing initial funding is often one of the most significant challenges during the early stages of a startup. Entrepreneurs must be resourceful and proactive in seeking out potential investors or funding opportunities. Ahmed, for instance, leveraged his professional network to connect with angel investors who believed in his vision for a renewable energy solution. His ability to secure early-stage funding was instrumental in turning his concept into a reality.

Building a startup's foundation also involves establishing a clear business model and strategy. Entrepreneurs must define how their product or service will generate revenue and achieve sustainability. When Sophia launched her online marketplace, she spent considerable time analyzing different revenue models and market strategies. Her thorough planning and strategic approach enabled her to create a scalable and profitable business.

The foundation phase is often marked by a steep learning curve. Entrepreneurs must be willing to learn from their mistakes and adapt quickly to changing circumstances. James, who founded an AI-driven marketing platform, encountered numerous setbacks during the initial development phase. However, his openness to feedback and willingness to pivot allowed him to overcome these challenges and build a robust foundation for his startup.

4

Chapter 4: Facing Adversity

In the startup world, adversity is a constant companion. Every entrepreneur faces obstacles that test their resolve and creativity. Overcoming these challenges is often what separates successful startups from those that falter. For Rachel, the founder of a biotech company, the journey was fraught with regulatory hurdles and technical difficulties. Her relentless pursuit of solutions and her ability to rally her team around a common goal exemplify the resilience required to navigate adversity.

Financial constraints are one of the most common challenges startups face. Many entrepreneurs bootstrap their ventures, relying on personal savings and limited resources. For example, Ben, who founded a cybersecurity startup, had to carefully manage his finances while developing his product. His story highlights the importance of financial discipline and the ability to make strategic decisions under pressure.

Market competition is another significant challenge for startups. Entrepreneurs must constantly innovate and differentiate their offerings to stay ahead. Olivia, the founder of an e-commerce platform, faced fierce competition from established players. Her ability to identify unique market opportunities and adapt her business model enabled her to carve out a niche in the crowded marketplace.

The emotional toll of running a startup can also be substantial. Entrepreneurs often work long hours and face immense pressure to succeed.

David, who started a mental health app, experienced burnout during the early stages of his venture. His journey underscores the importance of self-care and seeking support from mentors and peers. Balancing personal well-being with professional responsibilities is crucial for long-term success.

Legal and regulatory challenges can pose significant obstacles for startups, particularly in highly regulated industries. When Maria launched her fintech startup, she encountered numerous regulatory complexities. Her persistence in navigating these challenges and her ability to build relationships with key stakeholders were instrumental in overcoming these barriers.

Adversity often serves as a catalyst for innovation and growth. Entrepreneurs who embrace challenges and view them as opportunities for learning and improvement are more likely to succeed. Daniel, the founder of a clean energy startup, faced multiple setbacks in developing his technology. However, his unwavering commitment to his vision and his ability to pivot and adapt ultimately led to breakthroughs that propelled his startup forward.

5

Chapter 5: The Growth Phase

The growth phase of a startup is a thrilling period marked by rapid expansion and new opportunities. After establishing a solid foundation, entrepreneurs shift their focus to scaling their operations and increasing their market reach. For many, this phase involves securing additional funding, expanding the team, and enhancing their product or service offerings. Emily, the founder of a tech startup, experienced exponential growth after a successful round of Series A funding. This influx of capital allowed her to hire top talent and accelerate product development, propelling her startup to new heights.

Strategic planning is crucial during the growth phase. Entrepreneurs must carefully manage resources, set clear goals, and develop strategies to achieve them. Alex, who founded an online education platform, emphasizes the importance of having a well-defined growth plan. By setting measurable milestones and continuously evaluating progress, he was able to stay on track and make informed decisions that contributed to his startup's sustained growth.

Expanding the customer base is a key objective during the growth phase. This often involves exploring new markets and reaching a broader audience. When Sarah, the founder of a health and wellness app, identified an untapped market segment, she tailored her marketing efforts to target this new audience. Her ability to adapt and expand her customer base played a significant role in her startup's success.

As startups grow, maintaining company culture becomes increasingly important. A strong, positive culture can drive employee engagement, productivity, and overall success. Jessica, who scaled her fashion startup to an international brand, focused on nurturing a culture of creativity and collaboration. By prioritizing employee well-being and fostering a sense of belonging, she ensured that her team remained motivated and aligned with the company's vision.

The growth phase also presents challenges, such as managing increased operational complexity and maintaining product quality. Entrepreneurs must develop robust systems and processes to handle the demands of a growing business. Michael, the founder of a logistics startup, implemented scalable solutions to streamline operations and ensure consistent service delivery. His proactive approach to managing growth allowed his startup to thrive without compromising on quality.

Innovation remains a critical factor during the growth phase. Startups must continue to evolve and adapt to stay competitive. Nina, the founder of a social media platform, regularly invested in research and development to enhance her product offerings and stay ahead of industry trends. Her commitment to innovation enabled her startup to remain relevant and attract a loyal user base.

6

Chapter 6: Innovation and Adaptation

In the ever-evolving world of startups, continuous innovation and adaptation are essential for long-term success. Entrepreneurs must be proactive in identifying opportunities for improvement and staying ahead of market trends. For David, the founder of a fintech startup, innovation was at the core of his company's growth strategy. By leveraging cutting-edge technology and embracing a culture of experimentation, he was able to create a product that disrupted the traditional banking industry.

Listening to customer feedback is a crucial component of innovation. Startups must be attuned to the needs and preferences of their users to refine their products and services. Maria, the founder of a fitness app, prioritized user feedback and incorporated it into her development process. This iterative approach allowed her to create a product that resonated with her audience and kept them engaged.

Adapting to market changes is another critical aspect of innovation. Entrepreneurs must be agile and responsive to shifts in consumer behavior and industry trends. When Olivia, the founder of an e-commerce platform, noticed a growing demand for sustainable products, she quickly adapted her offerings to include eco-friendly options. Her ability to pivot and respond to market trends ensured her startup's continued success.

Collaboration and partnerships can also drive innovation. Startups can benefit from working with other organizations, sharing knowledge, and co-developing solutions. Alex, who founded a biotech company, formed strategic partnerships with research institutions to advance his product development. These collaborations provided access to new resources and expertise, accelerating his startup's innovation efforts.

Fostering a culture of innovation within the company is essential. Entrepreneurs must encourage creativity, experimentation, and a willingness to take risks. Sarah, the founder of a tech startup, implemented regular brainstorming sessions and hackathons to inspire her team and generate new ideas. Her commitment to fostering innovation created an environment where employees felt empowered to contribute to the company's growth.

Finally, staying informed about industry developments and emerging technologies is crucial for maintaining a competitive edge. Entrepreneurs must continuously educate themselves and their teams to stay ahead of the curve. When Mark, the founder of a renewable energy startup, recognized the potential of a new technology, he quickly integrated it into his product offerings. His proactive approach to innovation ensured his startup's continued relevance in a rapidly changing industry.

7

Chapter 7: Building a Culture

The culture within a startup plays a pivotal role in its success. It encompasses the values, beliefs, and behaviors that define the work environment and influence how employees interact with one another. For many entrepreneurs, building a positive and inclusive culture is as important as developing their product or service. When Anna founded her tech company, she prioritized creating a culture of collaboration and innovation. By fostering an open and supportive environment, she encouraged her team to share ideas and take risks, driving the company's growth and success.

Communication is a cornerstone of a strong company culture. Entrepreneurs must establish clear and transparent communication channels to ensure that all team members are aligned with the company's vision and goals. When James started his marketing startup, he implemented regular team meetings and feedback sessions. This open communication culture allowed employees to voice their opinions and contribute to the company's strategic decisions, fostering a sense of ownership and accountability.

Diversity and inclusion are critical components of a thriving company culture. Entrepreneurs must actively seek to build diverse teams and create an environment where everyone feels valued and respected. Lisa, the founder of a health-tech startup, focused on hiring individuals from diverse backgrounds and ensuring that her company was inclusive and equitable. Her commitment to diversity not only enriched the company's culture but also drove innovation by bringing different perspectives to the table.

Work-life balance is another essential aspect of a positive company culture. Entrepreneurs must recognize the importance of employee well-being and create policies that support a healthy work-life balance. When David founded his fintech startup, he implemented flexible working hours and encouraged employees to take time off when needed. This focus on well-being helped reduce burnout and increased overall productivity and job satisfaction.

Recognition and reward systems are vital for maintaining motivation and morale within a startup. Entrepreneurs must acknowledge and celebrate the achievements and contributions of their team members. Sarah, the founder of an e-commerce platform, implemented a recognition program that highlighted outstanding performance and rewarded employees with bonuses and other incentives. This system of recognition helped build a culture of appreciation and motivated employees to strive for excellence.

Finally, leadership plays a crucial role in shaping and sustaining company culture. Entrepreneurs must lead by example and embody the values they wish to instill in their teams. Alex, the founder of a renewable energy startup, demonstrated his commitment to sustainability by implementing eco-friendly practices within the company and encouraging employees to do the same. His leadership set the tone for the company's culture and inspired employees to align with the company's mission and values.

8

Chapter 8: The Role of Mentorship

Mentorship is a vital element in the journey of many successful startups. Experienced mentors provide guidance, support, and valuable connections that can significantly impact a startup's trajectory. For many entrepreneurs, finding the right mentor can make the difference between success and failure. When Emily started her tech company, she sought out a mentor with extensive industry experience. This mentor provided invaluable advice on product development and market strategy, helping Emily navigate the challenges of the startup world.

Mentors offer a wealth of knowledge and experience that can help entrepreneurs avoid common pitfalls. David, the founder of a health-tech startup, credits much of his success to the guidance of his mentor, who had previously founded a successful company in the same field. By sharing their experiences and lessons learned, mentors help entrepreneurs make informed decisions and develop effective strategies.

The emotional support provided by mentors is also crucial. The startup journey can be lonely and stressful, and having a mentor to turn to for encouragement and advice can make a significant difference. Jessica, who founded a fashion brand, often relied on her mentor for emotional support during challenging times. This support helped her stay motivated and focused on her goals, even when faced with setbacks.

Mentorship also provides valuable networking opportunities. Mentors often have extensive professional networks and can introduce entrepreneurs to potential investors, partners, and customers. When Mark started his renewable energy company, his mentor connected him with key industry players who later became crucial partners in his venture. These connections provided Mark with the resources and support needed to grow his startup.

The relationship between a mentor and an entrepreneur is mutually beneficial. Mentors gain satisfaction from sharing their knowledge and contributing to the success of a new generation of entrepreneurs. Additionally, they often gain fresh perspectives and new ideas from their mentees, enriching their own professional experiences. For Rachel, who mentors several young entrepreneurs, the relationship is a source of inspiration and personal growth.

Building a successful mentorship relationship requires effort and commitment from both parties. Entrepreneurs must be proactive in seeking out mentors, open to feedback, and willing to learn. Mentors, in turn, must be dedicated to providing support and guidance, and willing to invest time and effort in their mentees' success. By fostering strong mentorship relationships, entrepreneurs can navigate the complexities of the startup world with greater confidence and success.

9

Chapter 9: Making a Social Impact

Modern startups are increasingly focusing on making a positive social impact alongside achieving business success. Entrepreneurs are driven not only by profit but also by a desire to contribute to society and address pressing global issues. For instance, when Rachel founded her social enterprise, she was motivated by her passion for addressing food insecurity in underserved communities. Her startup developed a sustainable business model that provided nutritious meals to those in need, demonstrating that businesses can be both profitable and socially responsible.

Integrating social responsibility into a startup's mission can enhance its brand value and attract like-minded customers and investors. John, the founder of an eco-friendly consumer goods company, built his brand around sustainability. By prioritizing environmentally friendly practices and products, he was able to attract a loyal customer base that valued his company's commitment to the planet. His success underscores the potential for startups to drive positive change while achieving commercial success.

Social impact initiatives often require collaboration with various stakeholders, including non-profit organizations, government agencies, and local communities. When Sophia launched her health-tech startup, she partnered with community health centers to provide affordable healthcare solutions. These partnerships not only amplified the impact of her work but also helped her gain valuable insights and resources. Collaboration and community engagement are essential components of creating meaningful social impact.

Transparency and accountability are crucial for startups aiming to make a social impact. Entrepreneurs must clearly communicate their mission, goals, and the impact of their initiatives to stakeholders. Olivia, who founded a fair-trade fashion brand, prioritized transparency in her supply chain and business practices. By openly sharing her company's efforts to promote ethical fashion, she built trust with customers and investors, reinforcing her brand's commitment to social responsibility.

Measuring and evaluating the impact of social initiatives is vital for continuous improvement and credibility. Entrepreneurs must develop metrics and systems to track their progress and make data-driven decisions. Alex, the founder of an education tech startup, implemented rigorous evaluation methods to assess the effectiveness of his programs in improving student outcomes. This commitment to measuring impact enabled him to refine his offerings and demonstrate the tangible benefits of his work to stakeholders.

Finally, startups that prioritize social impact can inspire and influence others to follow suit. By setting an example of how businesses can contribute to societal well-being, entrepreneurs can drive broader change within their industries. Mark, the founder of a clean energy startup, actively advocated for sustainable business practices and shared his knowledge with other entrepreneurs. His leadership and advocacy efforts helped promote a culture of social responsibility within the business community.

10

Chapter 10: Navigating the Global Stage

As startups grow, many seek to expand beyond their home markets and reach a global audience. International expansion presents both opportunities and challenges that entrepreneurs must navigate with careful planning and strategy. For many, entering new markets involves understanding and adapting to different cultural, economic, and regulatory environments. When Emily decided to take her tech startup global, she invested significant time in researching and understanding the target markets. This thorough preparation enabled her to tailor her product and marketing strategies to resonate with international customers.

One of the primary challenges of global expansion is navigating regulatory complexities in different countries. Entrepreneurs must comply with various legal and regulatory requirements, which can be time-consuming and costly. When David expanded his fintech startup to multiple countries, he encountered numerous regulatory hurdles. By working closely with legal experts and local partners, he successfully navigated these challenges and established a strong international presence.

Cultural differences can also impact a startup's success in foreign markets. Entrepreneurs must be sensitive to local customs, preferences, and business practices. Lisa, the founder of a health-tech startup, emphasizes the importance of cultural competence in international expansion. By understanding and respecting the cultural nuances of her target markets, she was able to build strong relationships with customers and partners, driving her startup's success abroad.

Building a global brand requires effective communication and marketing strategies. Entrepreneurs must develop messaging that resonates with diverse audiences while maintaining a consistent brand identity. When Sarah expanded her e-commerce platform internationally, she adapted her marketing campaigns to reflect the values and preferences of each market. This localized approach helped her connect with customers on a deeper level and build a loyal global following.

Strategic partnerships can play a crucial role in successful international expansion. Collaborating with local businesses and organizations can provide valuable market insights, resources, and support. When Alex expanded his renewable energy startup to new regions, he formed partnerships with local energy companies and government agencies. These collaborations facilitated market entry and helped him navigate the complexities of operating in foreign markets.

Finally, scaling operations to support global expansion requires robust infrastructure and processes. Entrepreneurs must ensure that their supply chains, logistics, and customer support systems can handle the demands of international growth. John, the founder of an eco-friendly consumer goods company, invested in scalable solutions and technologies to streamline his global operations. This proactive approach enabled him to deliver consistent quality and service to customers worldwide.

11

Chapter 11: The Exit Strategy

As startups mature, many reach a stage where founders and investors begin considering exit strategies. These strategies can vary widely, including mergers, acquisitions, and initial public offerings (IPOs). Each option presents its own set of opportunities and challenges, and the decision to pursue a particular exit strategy is often influenced by the startup's goals, market conditions, and long-term vision. When Michael, the founder of a health-tech company, decided to pursue an acquisition, he carefully evaluated potential buyers to ensure alignment with his company's mission and values.

Mergers and acquisitions (M&A) are common exit strategies for startups looking to join forces with larger companies or other startups. The process involves extensive negotiations, due diligence, and the integration of teams and operations. When Lisa's fintech startup was acquired by a major financial institution, she focused on ensuring a smooth transition for her employees and customers. Her experience underscores the importance of thorough preparation and effective communication during the M&A process.

Initial public offerings (IPOs) are another popular exit strategy, allowing startups to raise capital by selling shares to the public. Going public can provide significant financial rewards and increase a company's visibility and credibility. However, the IPO process is complex and demanding, requiring rigorous financial reporting, regulatory compliance, and investor relations.

When Sarah's e-commerce platform went public, she navigated the IPO process with the help of experienced advisors and a dedicated team. Her story highlights the importance of careful planning and expert guidance in achieving a successful IPO.

Some startups may choose to remain private and focus on long-term growth without pursuing an exit strategy. For Alex, the founder of a renewable energy startup, maintaining control and staying true to his mission were more important than seeking an exit. By prioritizing sustainable growth and reinvesting profits into the business, he continued to expand his company's impact and reach. His approach demonstrates that an exit strategy is not always necessary for a startup's success.

The decision to pursue an exit strategy is often influenced by the interests of investors. Venture capitalists and angel investors typically expect a return on their investment within a certain timeframe. Entrepreneurs must balance these expectations with their own vision and goals for the company. When Mark faced pressure from investors to pursue an exit, he carefully considered their perspectives while staying true to his mission. His ability to navigate these complex dynamics ultimately led to a mutually beneficial outcome.

Finally, the emotional and personal aspects of exiting a startup can be significant. Entrepreneurs often invest years of hard work and passion into their ventures, and the decision to exit can be bittersweet. Jessica, who sold her fashion brand, experienced a mix of emotions as she transitioned out of the company she had built from the ground up. Her journey highlights the importance of acknowledging and addressing the personal impact of an exit strategy, ensuring a smooth and positive transition for all involved.

12

Chapter 12: Reflections and Legacy

The final chapter of "Wired Destinies: The Personal Journeys Behind Global Startups" reflects on the journeys of entrepreneurs and the lasting legacies they leave behind. These stories of innovation, resilience, and impact serve as an inspiration to future generations of entrepreneurs. As we look back on the experiences of these founders, we gain a deeper understanding of the profound influence they have had on their industries, communities, and the world at large.

Entrepreneurs often reflect on the lessons they have learned throughout their journeys. For Emily, the founder of a tech startup, the importance of resilience and adaptability stands out as a key takeaway. Her experiences navigating challenges and pivoting in response to market changes have shaped her approach to business and life. By sharing these insights, Emily hopes to inspire other entrepreneurs to persevere in the face of adversity.

The impact of a successful startup extends beyond financial success and market share. Many entrepreneurs take pride in the positive social and environmental contributions their companies have made. When David reflects on his journey with his fintech startup, he is most proud of the increased financial inclusion and empowerment his platform has brought to underserved communities. His story underscores the potential for startups to drive meaningful change and leave a lasting legacy.

The relationships and networks built throughout the entrepreneurial journey are another significant aspect of a founder's legacy. Entrepreneurs often form deep connections with mentors, investors, employees, and customers. For Lisa, the founder of a health-tech startup, these relationships have been a source of support, inspiration, and collaboration. Her ability to build and nurture these connections has been instrumental in her success and continues to shape her professional journey.

Looking ahead, many entrepreneurs remain committed to fostering innovation and supporting the next generation of startups. Sarah, who successfully exited her e-commerce platform, now dedicates her time to mentoring young entrepreneurs and investing in new ventures. Her passion for innovation and her desire to give back to the entrepreneurial community reflect her enduring commitment to driving progress and supporting others on their journeys.

Finally, the legacy of a startup is often defined by the lasting impact it has on its industry and society. The entrepreneurs featured in this book have left an indelible mark through their groundbreaking innovations, dedication to social responsibility, and relentless pursuit of their visions. As we celebrate their achievements, we are reminded of the transformative power of entrepreneurship and the potential for individuals to shape the future.

Book Description: Wired Destinies: The Personal Journeys Behind Global Startups

In "Wired Destinies: The Personal Journeys Behind Global Startups," you'll embark on a captivating exploration of the entrepreneurial spirit that drives some of the most innovative and influential startups of our time. This book delves into the personal stories of founders, shedding light on the inspiration, challenges, and triumphs that have shaped their journeys from humble beginnings to global success.

Each chapter takes you through a different phase of the startup lifecycle, offering a unique blend of real-life anecdotes, practical insights, and valuable lessons. From the initial spark of an idea to the bold leap of faith, and from building a strong foundation to navigating adversity, you'll witness the resilience and determination that define successful entrepreneurs.

CHAPTER 12: REFLECTIONS AND LEGACY

As you move through the chapters, you'll uncover the critical moments that tested these founders' resolve and the strategies they employed to overcome obstacles. The growth phase reveals the meticulous planning and execution required to scale operations, while the innovation and adaptation chapter highlights the importance of staying ahead in a rapidly evolving market.

The book also delves into the cultural aspects of startups, emphasizing the significance of fostering a positive and inclusive work environment. You'll learn about the vital role of mentorship in guiding and supporting entrepreneurs, and the impact of startups that aim to make a positive social contribution.

The journey doesn't end there. "Wired Destinies" takes you beyond the local market, exploring the challenges and opportunities of global expansion. Finally, you'll discover the various exit strategies that startups may pursue and reflect on the lasting legacies these entrepreneurs leave behind.

"Wired Destinies: The Personal Journeys Behind Global Startups" is more than just a collection of startup success stories. It's a tribute to the ingenuity, passion, and perseverance of entrepreneurs who dare to dream big and change the world. Whether you're an aspiring entrepreneur, a seasoned business leader, or simply someone intrigued by the world of startups, this book offers a wealth of inspiration and knowledge to fuel your own journey.

www.ingramcontent.com/pod-product-compliance
Lightning Source LLC
LaVergne TN
LVHW020744090526
838202LV00057BA/6229